Cou

1

Wirral & West Cheshire

Seddon Neudorfer

Publishing Ltd

www.countrysidedogwalks.co.uk

First published in July 2013 by **Wet Nose Publishing Ltd**,
Summer Roost
Graigfechan
Denbighshire
LL15 2EU
All enquiries regarding sales telephone: 01824 704398
email cdw@wetnosepublishing.co.uk
www.countrysidedogwalks.co.uk
ISBN 978-0-9573722-4-5

We would like to thank everyone who has helped us, especially:
Gloria Bedford, Dawn and John Marriott, Lucy and Adam Seddon,
Daisy Gibbs, Joanna and Andy Calveley, George and Flis Calveley,
Vicky and Bridget Gladstone, Lilly and her family, Bronson and his
family, Shirley and Jean.

Contents

Introduction 1

1. Bidston Hill - (Easy)...5

2. Caldy Hill - (Easy)..9

3. Royden Park - (Easy)...13

4. Arrowe Park - (Easy)..19

5. Thurstaston - (Easy)...23

6. Heswall Dales - (Easy)..27

7. Dibbinsdale - (Easy)...31

8. Eastham - (Easy)..35

9. Parkgate - (Medium)..39

10. Rivacre Valley - (Easy)..43

11. River Dee - (Medium)..45

12. Helsby - (Medium)..51

13. Frodsham - (Medium)..55

14. Delamere Forest - (Easy).......................................61

15. Marbury Park - (Medium).......................................65

16. Bickerton Hill - (Medium).......................................69

17. Little Budworth - (Easy)...75

18. Whitegate Way - (Easy)...79

19. Little Leigh - (Easy)..83

20. River Weaver - (Easy)...87

Introduction

The twenty walks included in this book are all designed so that you and your wet nosed friend have a really enjoyable time. Where there are stiles, they are specially designed with lift gates for dogs. At a quick glance there is information at the beginning of each walk to tell you what to expect and what you may need to take with you. The descriptive guides will also warn of any roads ahead or areas of livestock so that you can get your dog on the lead well in advance.

Dogs just love to explore new places. They really enjoy the new smells and carry themselves a little higher with the added excitement. Going to new places gets you and your dog out and about, meeting new people and their dogs. It is important to socialise dogs, as they will be more likely to act in a friendly manner towards other dogs as they gain confidence.

The stunning pictures in this book are just a taster of what you can see along the way. Most of the walks are crammed with fantastic views and you are never far from water or woodlands: the latter will provide shade in the summer and shelter on cold, wet days where your dog will love the freedom to run up and down.

The walks are graded Easy, Medium and Challenging. They are all around one to three hours long, depending on your and your dog's pace. You may start with the easy ones and work up to the challenging walks depending on your and your dog's fitness. Different dog breeds and dog age must be taken into account when you decide which walks to do.

Different breeds of dog have different levels of fitness. For example, bulldogs can only do short walks whereas a border collie or a springer spaniel are extremely energetic and difficult to tire out. It is recommended that you do some research on the breed of dog that you own to get to know what sort of exercise that they require.

You may have a walk that you are happy doing with your dog every day, but this book will show you new areas to explore with a change of scenery and a chance to meet new people and their dogs. Dogs love new places to visit

and you will see the change in them as they explore the new surroundings, taking in the new smells with delight. You will fulfil both your life and your dog's just by trying somewhere new.

The Delamere Forest, Eastham Wood, and Royden Park walks are in the shade of the trees and are great for hot days, as many dogs don't cope well in the sun.

Some of the walks include bridleways, so you may encounter horses. It is important to put your dog on a lead if you see horses approach. It is always helpful to say hello to the riders as they near so that the horse realises that you are not a threat.

Ticks

If you have been walking in areas where sheep graze you should check your dog for ticks. They must be removed as soon as possible. It is best to use tick tweezers, which are specially designed to remove the head and leg parts of the tick. Ticks can carry diseases and the longer they remain latched on to your dog the more the chance of spreading infections.

Please clean up after your dog

Always be prepared, having dog bags with you at all times. Once you have cleaned up after your dog, please keep the bag, until you see a bin. If there are no bins provided, then take it away with you to a roadside bin. Dog bags that are discarded on the paths or in the bushes are unpleasant and unsightly and will not degrade.

Livestock

If you find that you need to cross a field with cattle or horses and they seem interested in you or your dog it is recommended within the Countryside Code to let your dog off the lead. Never try to get between livestock and your dog. Your dog will get out of a situation a lot more easily with speed than you can. It is usually only cattle with young calves that are a threat, or young heifers or bullocks that tend to get a little inquisitive. They will usually stop when they get close to you or your dog.

Most horses will come over for a fuss but a small proportion do have a problem with dogs. They may see them as a threat and will act to defend the herd. Horses that are out with a rider are completely different as they are not defending the herd, and as long as you keep a safe distance there should not be a problem.

Sheep are not a danger to you, but your dog can be a danger to them. Where sheep are grazing it is vital that you have your dog on a lead or under very close control. You will know your dog, but if you are unsure it is better to play safe and keep your dog on a lead. It is important always to have your dog on a lead when around lambs. Lambs have a higher pitched bleat and are about the size of a cat, and your dog may act differently amongst them.

Does your dog fetch a stick?

Most dogs love sticks and will pick them up without any encouragement from their owners. Vets and dog trainers recommend that you should not throw sticks for dogs. They can cause nasty injuries, sometimes fatal as the stick can pierce the throat, or rebound off the ground and cause harm to your dog.

Rivers

Some dogs love water and will think nothing of plunging into the river. With the extreme weather conditions over the last few years, a river that may be safe for your dog to swim in can change in a matter of hours to become a swollen torrent that could wash your dog away. Please be careful when near rivers if there have been heavy periods of rain or if they look swollen or fast flowing. It is best to put your dogs on the lead, until you have assessed the situation.

1. Bidston

Easy - 1.2 miles - 1hr

This is a super walk through stunning woodland and heathland, with lots of gorse adding lots of bright yellow flowers with a coconut smell. You will see a lot of exposed sandstone, and a windmill, built in the 1800s. The furthest point of the walk has a view of a famous landmark, the observatory, which was built in 1866 out of sandstone excavated on site. There are also ancient carvings of a sun goddess just before the observatory. There are no livestock and just a brief section of road.

How to get there - Take Junction 1 off the M53, follow signs for Birkenhead on the A553, and then follow the brown signs for Tam O'Shanters Farm Park turning right onto the B5151 Boundary Road. On reaching the farm park the car park will be found just after the entrance on your left.

Grid Reference - SJ 291893
Postcode - CH43 7PD

Parking - Free in the car parky

Facilities - There are no facilities

You will need - Dog lead, dog bags, water for your dog

The Walk

❶ From the car park, face the green and take the path to the left, signed for the windmill. Follow the path with the green to your right. Once you meet another path cross this to go straight ahead through the mixed woodland. Ignore the minor paths on your left and right and continue where you will see a boundary fence. Walk with the boundary fence on your left.

When you meet a fork in the path take the right path and continue through the woods. The path becomes unclear for a short section as the trees become more widely spaced. You will see a boundary sandstone wall ahead.

Head for the boundary wall; once near to it, turn right following the wall, passing rhododendron on your right. You will reach another path with exposed sandstone bedrock; turn left onto this path, which brings

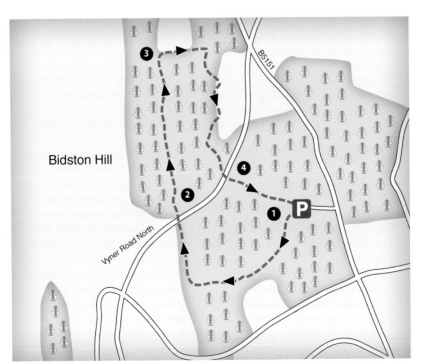

you out of the woodland and into heathland. The heathland is dominated by gorse here but it is still very pleasant.

Follow the path between the gorse, stepping onto exposed bedrock, where you will soon see the windmill ahead. Stay on the sandstone path, and on meeting another path turn right. ❷ You will reach a bridge ahead where you cross over the road below.

Pass the windmill, keeping to the exposed bedrock with gorse and trees to both sides. You will pass a toposcope, where there were once views before the trees grew up.

A little further along you will have views both left and right. To the left, you can see across the Wirral and the river Dee to North Wales. On the right the view looks over Birkenhead, to Liverpool.

Go straight ahead now, where you will see the beautiful Observatory building. Somewhere before reaching the boundary wall there is an ancient rock carving of a Sun Goddess. Take care that your dog doesn't jump the boundary wall, as there is quite a drop on the other side. On reaching near to the wall turn right.

❸ Descend the steps and continue on the path with the sandstone wall on your left and then when you meet with a fork take the right path. Once you reach another path turn right. The woodland here is dominated by oak and silver birch with gorse and pockets of heather. Ignore minor paths and continue straight ahead, walking over exposed sandstone bedrock.

You will pass a small section of sandstone wall to your left; the path follows remnants of the wall to ground level. Just before reaching back into the open heath, take a path on the left over stone slabs from the old wall. Put your dog on a lead now as there is a road ahead.

You will reach a worn path ahead: turn right here, heading towards the road. Pass through the entrance, then turn left and cross the road after the bend. Follow the footpath way marker back into the woodland and continue straight ahead following the obvious worn path. You will reach another path: cross this and continue straight ahead. You will soon see the car park.

2. Caldy Hill

Easy - 1.6 miles - 1hr

This is a fantastic walk, starting in the lovely mixed broadleaved woodland known as Stapleton Woods. It then continues into Caldy Hill, which is a mix of oak and silver birch woodland and heathland. There are fantastic views over the River Dee to North Wales. Hilbre Island and West Kirby Marina can also be viewed from the toposcope. Your dog will love running around in the woodlands and searching through the scrub areas. There are no roads and no livestock to worry about.

How to get there - Parking for Caldy Hill is between West Kirby and Caldy. From West Kirby continue on the A540 heading for Heswall. Just after passing Caldy Grange Grammar School on your left, look out for a minor road on your right, King's Drive North. Parking will be found at the end of this road. If you reach Caldy roundabout you have missed your turning.

Grid Reference - SJ 229860

Parking - Free in the car park at the end of King's Drive North

Facilities - There are no facilities

You will need - Dog leads, dog bags, and water for your dog

The Walk

❶ From the car park, head away from the road and into the woods. Ignore a path immediately to your right and continue straight ahead. Ignore another path to your right. Take the next path on the left, which is indicated by a way marker.

Pass over a small hillock and continue straight ahead, ignoring a path on your right. Descend a small hill and on meeting another path turn right. The path will meet close to a field edge on your left. Follow parallel with the field. Ignore a path on your right and continue.

You will reach the field edge, with a sandstone wall. Ignore another path on the right and continue alongside the field. At the end of the field the path narrows. Turn right just before reaching an exit with steps. Ascend the path and ignore a path on the right, continuing to ascend.

Soon you will be walking beside gardens. Take the path to the right, veering away from the garden fence. Stay on this wider path, passing more gardens to your left. You will meet a path on the left and on the right. Take the path on the left. Again you will have gardens to your left a little further along.

Ignore a path on the right and continue, where the path ascends over sandstone bedrock. Call your dog close now, as there is a quiet road ahead. **❷** When you reach the head of a cul-de-sac to your left, pass over the bridleway and take the path straight ahead.

As the path bends to your left, stay on the wider path, ignoring a path to your right. You will again pass gardens on your left. Stay on the path, ignoring another path to the right just as you pass the gardens.

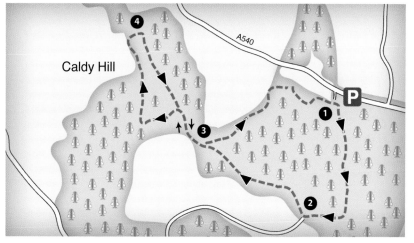

Ignore a path on your left and continue straight ahead, through predominantly oak and silver birch woodland with bracken, holly and rhododendron understory. Keep to the main path, ignoring any minor paths. ❸ On reaching a sandstone wall, pass through the gap, onto a bridleway, turning right.

Take the left path, passing again through a gap in the sandstone wall, and enter into Caldy Hill, passing under the large rhododendron. Take the left path, before an opening in the trees. Cross another path and continue straight ahead, ignoring a path on your left. You will be beside gardens once again on your left. The path veers to the left, where you will have heathland to your right and woods to your left. When you reach a bench on another path, turn right. You will now have views of the sea and across the estuary to North Wales.

Ignore a path on your left and continue passing heathland over sandstone bedrock. Stay to the left at the fork, passing between the gorse. You will soon enter back into the woods, passing a wet boggy area on your right. You will soon have garden fences once more on your left. Stay on the path, ignoring a path on your right. There is a lot of gorse, with mixed woodland and bracken.

Just before going up and over the sandstone bedrock, turn on the narrow path on your right. Ascend between gorse, passing a sandstone wall on your left. The area opens up, with sandstone bedrock, dominated by gorse. You will have views to your right across the estuary to North Wales and ahead there is a toposcope.

❹ Ascend the steps to the toposcope, where your view is extended. It is a beautiful sight, on a clear day. Hilbre Island can be seen, to the forefront of the estuary. With your back to the estuary, descend the steps ahead and to your right. Follow the path between the gorse and on reaching another path turn right.

Ignore another path on the right and continue back into the woodland, now dominated by oaks with gorse understory. The path will then open up into heathland once again. Continue on the path, crossing the heathland and then back into woodland. Cross a path and continue straight ahead.

Pass the tall rhododendron once again on a familiar path. Go through the gap in the stone wall and turn right, then pass through another gap once again back into mixed broadleaved woodland, known as Stapleton Wood. Turn almost immediately left, passing between hollies. You will have gardens on your left and ahead of you.

The path will then bend sharply to the right with gardens on your left and woodland to your right. Walk to the edge of the woods at first, and then you will be amongst coppiced woodland. When you reach two paths ahead take the path on the right. Continue straight ahead, where you will soon reach another path. Turn left here and head back towards your car.

3. Royden Park

Easy - 2.4 miles - 1hr

This is a lovely walk through beautiful broadleaved woodlands with some pines, rhododendrons and small areas of open heathland, which look stunning when in flower. There are no roads but on occasions there may be sheep grazing in parts of the walk. This walk is fantastic all year round but perfect for those hot days when dogs need to get out of the sun.

How to get there - From the A540 between West Kirby and Thurstaston, at the Caldy roundabout take the turn following for Frankby, and follow the brown signs to Royden Park on the B5140. At the end of this road turn right. Royden Park is ahead and to the right at the bend in the road.

Grid Reference - SJ 245857
Nearest Postcode - CH48 1NP

Parking - Free in the car park

Facilities - There are toilets, a café and a tap with bowl for dogs

You will need - Dog leads, dog bags

The Walk

❶ Starting at the toilet block, facing the car park, turn right and pass beside a vehicle barrier, following signs for Roodee Mere along the access drive. Ignore the gates on the left and continue on the path where you cross the model railway.

Continue on the path with Roodee Mere to your left, putting dogs on leads to ensure they don't enter the water, as this is a by-law of the park. Follow the railway on your right. Ignore a path on the right and follow the path which bends to the left, signed Thurstaston Woods.

You will now be walking in mixed woodland with rhododendron, with chestnut paling on your left. Just before the end of the chestnut paling, the path bends to the right, becoming a little unclear. You will reach near to a boundary fence on your far left. Continue on this path passing the edge of a stone boundary wall. Turn right here and continue, where you will reach another boundary wall ahead. You will now leave Royden Park and enter Thurstaston Woods.

Take the well worn path, keeping the stone wall on your right. On reaching the end of the wall, turn left.

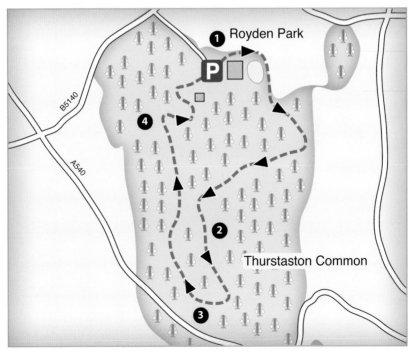

Follow the obvious path through the woodland, passing an interpretation panel to your right, as you enter Thurstaston Common, which is owned and managed by the National Trust.

The woods will clear, and you will be walking amongst open heathland, which is a glorious sight when the heather is in flower. Take care here to keep your dog under close control, keeping to the path in the months of March to July as there may be ground nesting birds.

You will now enter back into woodland, and on meeting with another path, turn right on this path and go through the kissing gate. If sheep are grazing ensure you have close control of your dog. There will be a sign on the gate if sheep are present. Gorse is dominant here, and although not desired by heathland managers, it looks stunning when in bloom, and has a coconut fragrance. There may be ground nesting birds in this section also.

Follow the stone track, taking a path on your right, just before Benty's Farm. You will pass a boggy area to your left. Then pass through a lift gate. Continue straight ahead and to your left. You will pass a large sandstone outcrop on your left known as Thor's Stone. ❷

Go to the end of the stone and ignore the narrow path straight ahead. Follow the path to the left, around the end of the stone, and turn immediately right. On reaching another path out in the open, turn right. ❸ You will have stunning views of the estuary and North Wales beyond on your left and will be on exposed bedrock with trees to your right. Stay on this path with the views to your left, ignoring any desire lines to your right.

The path will narrow as you walk between the gorse, with an expanse of heather along the slopes and below to your left. You will reach the edge of a sandstone block. You can take a path just before this edge into the woods to avoid this large step down.

The path will now descend through oak and silver birch woodland. A little further on the path becomes unclear, but continue straight ahead, and on reaching the bottom of the hill the path will become more obvious. The woods will become less dense. There is a silver birch tree in the middle of the path - take a path straight ahead, but to your right here. It is not obvious at first. Immediately after this take another path to the right. ❹

You will see a sandstone wall to your left. Ignore a couple of minor tracks, which lead to entrances in the stone wall. Ignore a path to your right and then when you see the Tudor hall, which is Hill Bark Hotel, take a path on the left into Royden Park.

Take the path diagonally left with the hall on your far right. Trees and gorse with rhododendron surround the field edge. On reaching another path, turn left. Keep to this path, ignoring all other minor desire lines.

You will go back into the woods and when you reach the exposed rock take the path on the right. Continue with a bank on the left, passing between the rhododendrons. Cross an old boundary wall, then turn immediately right, walking amongst the rhododendron with Scots pines.

Ignore a path on the right and continue until you meet another path, then turn right. You will meet another wider path where you will need to put your dog on the lead. Ignore the gate opposite and turn right once more. Follow this path and go through the gap next to the gate, passing a parking bay on the left and crossing an access road where you will meet with the car park and toilet block.

4. Arrowe Park

Easy - 2 miles - 1hr

This is a pleasant walk under a canopy of mature broadleaved trees, following a stream for part of the walk where your dog will enjoy splashing about. Mid-way along there are open areas where your dog may enjoy a game of fetch, or find other dogs to play with. There is a fishing lake, which is enclosed so you can enjoy watching the wildfowl without your dog chasing them off. To the fisherman's dismay you may glimpse a cormorant, out to steal the fish.

How to get there - Take Junction 3 off the M53, follow signs for Arrowe Park Hospital, passing the hospital on the left, and pass the car park for Arrowe Country Park and golf course, again on your left. Take the next left turn onto Arrowe Brook road and you will find the car park on the left hand side of the road a little further down, just before reaching Arrowe Brook Lane.

Grid Reference - SJ 266868
Nearest Postcode - CH49 1SX

Parking - Free in the car park on Arrowe Brook Road

Facilities - There are no facilities on this walk

You will need - Dog leads, dog bags

Countryside Dog Walks - Wirral & West Cheshire

The Walk

❶ From the car park, pass through the barrier at the end furthest from the road, and follow the sealed path into the woodland. There is rhododendron to both sides of the path. At the bend you will reach a stream where your dog can cool off.

Just before you leave the woods into the opening ahead, take the wide path on the right that isn't surfaced, which stays within the woodland. Ignore the path on the right and continue straight ahead, passing between the dense rhododendron bushes.

Cross a bridge over the stream and follow a fence line on your left. Ignore the path on the left and continue, passing a fishing lake on your left.

❷ Continue to follow the fence line and at the end you will cross an old stone bridge.

Ignore a path on the left and continue through the mature woodland. The rhododendron clears here with the woodland

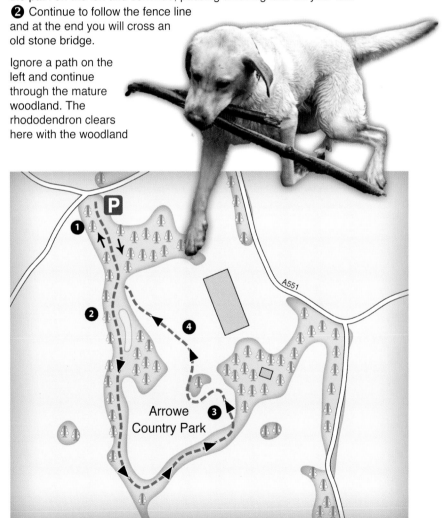

floor being more open. Ignore another path on the left and continue.

You will meet with another path, where you turn left, passing a golf course on the other side of the trees to your right. A little further along ignore paths to the left and right and continue through the oak-dominated woodland.

You will pass a pond on your left and then you will reach the thick rhododendron bushes once more. Ignore paths to the left and right again and continue. Pass a pond on the right, and on reaching a sealed path, turn left.

❸ A little further ahead, as you leave the canopy of the trees, you will pass a fenced play area to your right. Ignore the path on the right after the play area and then take the path on the left. Ignore a path on your right almost immediately and continue walking to the edge of the field. You will now be walking alongside trees and scrub.

You will pass an old stone gate post on your left. Once you reach the end of the trees turn right and join another large open area, where you can see a tall chimney to your right. Cross to the left hand side of this field with scrub to your left. Ignore a path to the left; you will then be walking alongside the woodland on your left. ❹

Continue to walk to the edge of the field. Further along you will meet a sealed path to your right. Join this path and continue in the same direction to leave the field. Once back in the woods you will soon be on a familiar path.

Continue on this sealed path where your dog will search out that stream once more. Retrace your steps back to the car park.

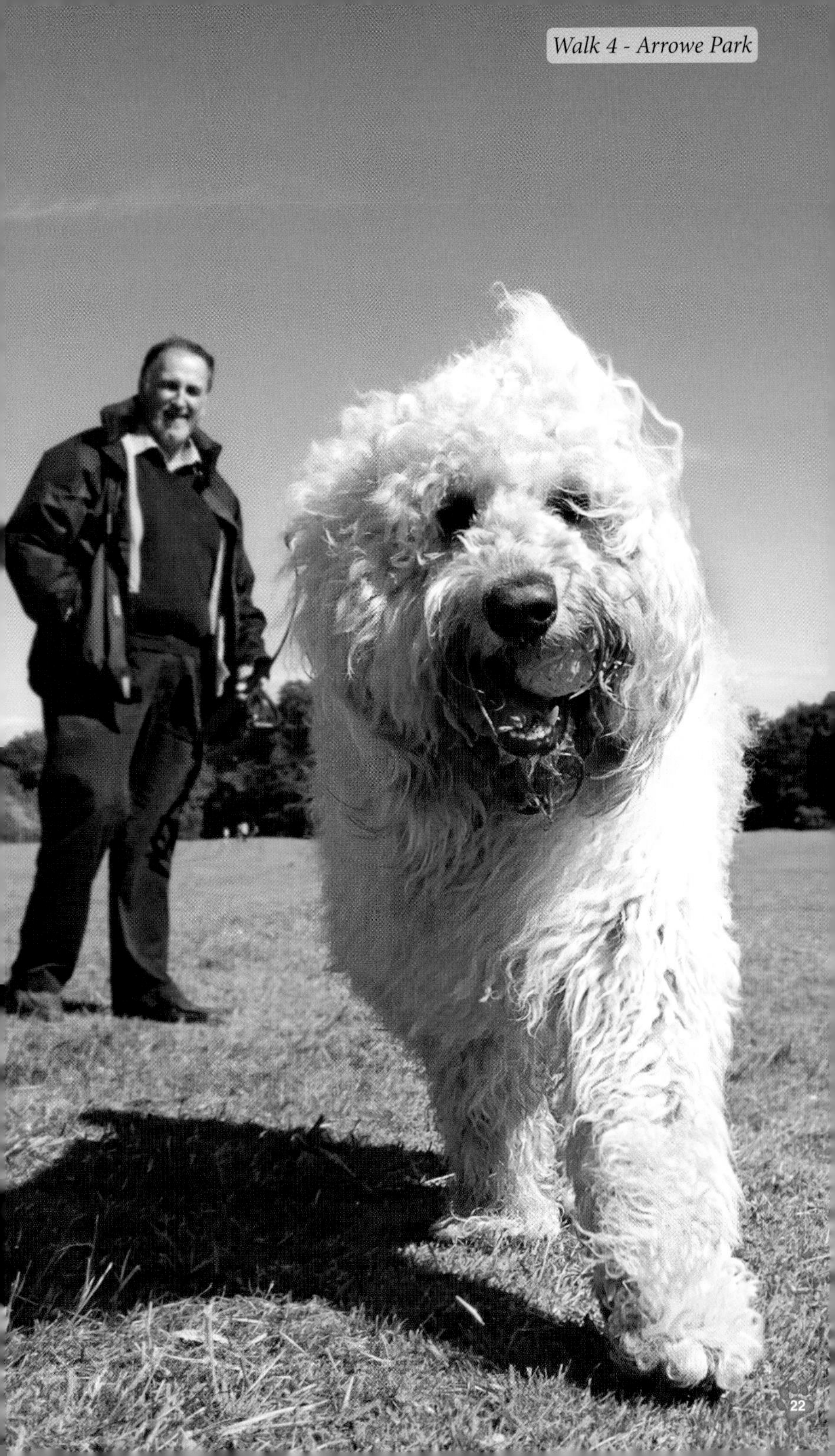

5. Thurstaston

Easy- 2.7 miles -1.5hr

This is a super walk, following part of the Wirral Way, an old disused railway line. There are stunning views across the estuary to North Wales. The walk crosses a lovely meadow, with a pond, passing between hedgerows and then a walk along the beach, before returning back to the car park. There are no roads and no livestock. Please note that during the spring high tides in March and October it is advised that you check and avoid high tide times. There is water for dogs at the visitor centre and the café at the beginning and end of the walk, and on entering the beach. Cyclists share the section of footpath along the Wirral Way.

How to get there - From Heswall follow signs for Hoylake on the A540 – Telegraph Road. Turn left at the roundabout once in Thurstaston, following the signs for Thurstaston Country Park on Station Road.

Grid Reference - SJ 239834
Postcode - CH61 0HN

Parking - Pay and Display

Facilities - There are toilets and a snack bar at the visitor centre and a café just as you approach the car park

You will need - Dog leads, dog bags

The Walk

❶ From the car park, go to the furthest end and take the gate to follow through the old campsite. Pass through another gate, entering on to the Wirral Way. You will have views on your right over the estuary to North Wales.

Pass under a bridge and continue along the path. Ignore a footpath on the left to the Dungeon. A little further along take the path on your right, signed for Heswall Fields. ❷ When reaching two gates, take the one on the left and head towards the estuary, between a stock fence and a hedge.

Ignore a left turn and pass through the gap, beside the gate. Turn immediately left here, to walk alongside a hedgerow, with the meadow on your right. You will pass a pond on your right. Continue on the worn, grassy path. Ignore a gate on your left and head towards the corner of the field. ❸

There is an exit here, and on leaving the meadow go straight ahead, between the hedgerows. Turn right to enter onto the beach and then turn right again. Your dog will find an inlet of fresh water here, as it enters into the sea.

Follow the estuary on your left, with marram grass and scrub on your right. You will pass sandy cliff faces and gorse scrub. Continue for a long stretch, passing a set of wooden steps on your right.

Head towards the white house in the distance. Just before reaching the house ascend a set of steps on your right, putting dogs on leads near the top, and then walk along a path between the hedgerows.

Pass between the bollards on the road and go through the gate on the right. Now head diagonally left, across the green, towards the pond and the visitor centre. Take the path on the right on reaching the pond, walking with the pond on your left. Continue ahead and to the left, where you will reach the car park.

6. Heswall Dales

Easy - 2miles - 1hr

This is a lovely walk with heathland, oak and birch woodland, sandstone bedrock and views over the River Dee to North Wales. There are gorse patches which smell wonderfully of coconut as you pass and basking common lizards, which scurry away as you approach. There are no livestock and only short sections of quiet road.

How to get there - From Chester take the A540, signed for Parkgate. On reaching Parkgate, stay on the A540 following signs for Hoylake. Just after passing Heswall village, staying on the A540, turn left onto Thurstaston Road. Turn right onto Oldfield Road and continue to the end of the road, turning left. Park on this road, just before Greenfield Lane.

Grid Reference - SJ 255827
Nearest Postcode - CH60 6SG

Parking - Free on the roadside

You will need - Dog leads, dog bags, and water for your dog

The Walk

❶ From the road, walk downhill towards Greenfield Lane. Take the byway to the left of Greenfield Lane. The road will bend to the left, just after passing the houses, take the narrow path on the left, ❷ which widens out as you ascend. You will pass between gorse, bracken and scattered trees.

Pass through an entrance and continue straight ahead, ignoring a path to the left and right. You will now have wonderful views on your right, across the heathland and over the River Dee to North Wales.

Ignore a path on your left, just after passing the stone bench, and continue straight ahead. The path will start to descend and on reaching a fork, turn right. The path is undulating with views again on your right, on the higher sections. You will still be walking amongst the heathland and gorse, with scattered oak and silver birch.

At a set of steps you will descend into silver birch woodland, turning left on meeting the path. ❸ A little further on, on meeting another path turn left. The path will ascend through oak and rowan trees, with holly and bracken understory. Ascend a couple of steps and continue straight ahead.

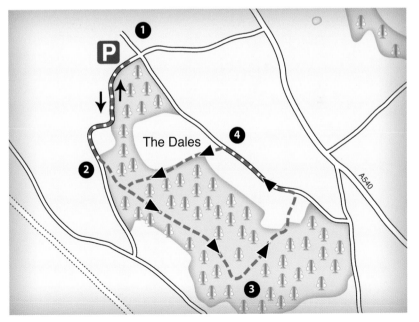

Take the path ahead and over to the right, which ascends with a couple of steps to begin with and then a set of steps as you climb. Pass some sandstone outcrops and then pass through a gap in the fence and turn right on the worn path. You will have heathland and bilberry on your right, and woodland with foxgloves in summer on your left. Pass a gate on your left.

The path is undulating once again, with views over the River Dee. Take the next path on the left, ascending the steps and then passing through the gap in the fence. The path will continue to ascend, passing over exposed sandstone bedrock once more, between gorse.

Put your dog on the lead as the path widens out and becomes wooded, as there is a road ahead. You will pass between gardens and on reaching the quiet road turn left. ❹ A little further along, turn left onto the quiet, narrow lane, signed for Dale Farm and Heswall Dales.

The lane will descend to reach the back entrance to Dale Farm on your left. Ignore this and pass through the squeeze post ahead and to your right. On passing Dale Farm you will have heathland to your left once more. You will have views once more straight ahead, and the path will descend. Ignore a path on your left and continue, where you will reach the exit once again.

Go out of the exit and continue on a familiar path through the vegetation and scrub. Ignore a minor path on the left and continue to the road. Turn right and pass the houses once more, where ascending now you will reach back to your car.

7. Dibbinsdale

Easy - 2 miles - 1hr

This is a beautiful walk amongst fantastic woodland, with meadows and marsh areas and lots of streams, ponds and a river. Your dog will love running up and down the wooded slopes and in the spring there are lots of flowers adding colour to the woodland floor.

How to get there - From the M53 junction 4 follow signs to Bebington on the B5137. Pass Spital train station on your right and then turn right at the roundabout. The car park will be found on the right hand side of the road.

Grid Reference - SJ 345827
Nearest Postcode - CH62 2AD

Parking - Free in the car park

Facilities - There are no facilities

You will need - Dog leads, dog bags

The Walk

❶ From the car park take the middle path which is signed for the Ranger's office. You will pass through mixed broadleaved woodland with meadow areas. Where the path meets a larger meadow take the path on the right, descending slightly with the meadow on your left.

You will soon be on the edge of woodland with views into the valley on the right. Ignore a path on the left heading back. The path will descend into the valley. On reaching the fenced ponds, turn right. At the fork in the path go left.

A little further along you will cross a bridge over a river, and once you are over the bridge you will pass a reed bed on your left. Take the path to your left and not the one going uphill. Continue alongside the reed bed with trees on each side of the path.

You will reach near to the water's edge where your dog can cool off. Continue with the water on your left and cross a bridge, then go through the tunnel underneath the railway. ❷

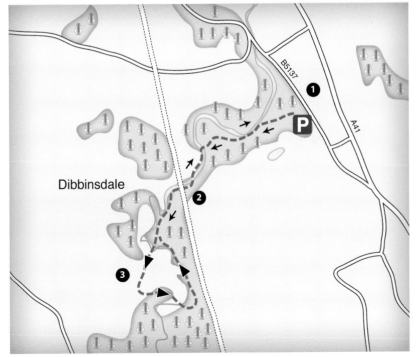

At the other end of the tunnel ignore the steps on the left and continue through the woodland. The path will ascend a little. Once the path levels out you will pass through a woodland clearing. Keep to the path, which follows the river, descending once again.

The path will level out and you will be walking close to the river. There are lots of bluebells and wood anemones in the woods in the spring, and marsh marigolds in the boggy area.

Cross a couple of bridges and stay on the main path, which brings you into a large meadow on your right and scrub to your left. ❸ Take the left fork at the end of the meadow. Continue between two bodies of water, cross a bridge over the river and go straight ahead ascending the steps, then turn left. Turn left again on a path, which ascends at first and then descends.

Looking to the left, you can see the oxbow in the river down below. On reaching another path, turn right and follow the path back the way you came to reach the tunnel once more.

Go out of the tunnel and back over the bridge, and turn right passing the reed bed. Cross the bridge and turn right; the path will ascend. When the path levels out, ignore a path on the right. The path will ascend once more. At the top of the hill follow the path to the left, which is at the edge of the valley on a main path. Turn left on reaching another path and follow this back to the car park.

8. Eastham Wood

Easy - 1.5 miles - 1hr

This is a fantastic woodland walk within Eastham Country Park, with bluebells and wood anemones in the spring, passing through the grounds of a Victorian zoo and pleasure garden with lots of mature rhododendrons. The bear pit still remains intact but thankfully the bears are wooden. There is an open grassland area where you can sit surrounded by gorse and silver birch, with a view across the river Mersey. There are no roads and no livestock.

How to get there - From the A41 between Ellesmere Port and Bebington look for the signs to Eastham Ferry and Country Park, taking Eastham Village Road and then Ferry Road. You will find Eastham Country Park on the left hand side.

Grid Reference - SJ 363818

Postcode - CH62 OBH

Parking - Free in the car park

Facilities - There are toilets, a visitor centre, a tearoom and a water tap and basin for dogs.

You will need - Dog leads, dog bags

The Walk

❶ From the car park head for the visitor centre, passing it on your left, and go through the gap beside the vehicle barrier. Go through the gateway and turn left into the mixed broadleaved woodland. Pass the tea garden on your left with a sandstone wall on your right and rhododendron bushes on both sides.

Take the path on the right, signed for the bear pit, and go straight ahead, descending the steps to the Victorian fountain. Pass the fountain and go up another set of steps to view the bear pit. This is the only enclosure remaining from a zoo housing a collection of exotic animals.

Passing the bear pit on your right with the fountain below and to your left, follow the path straight ahead. Ignore a path to the right, and when you reach another path turn right, passing stones on your right from the Victorian gardens.

Continue straight ahead until your reach square, stone gate posts. Don't go

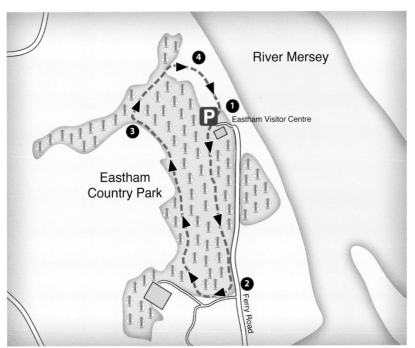

between the posts, but turn left. You will see a house through the trees ahead and you will reach another wider path. **❷** Turn right on this path, taking care: your dog can get onto a road that runs parallel with the path for a time as there are no boundary fences.

Ignore a path to the right and a little further you will pass an exit out of the park. Take care again to make sure your dog stays within the park and away from the road. Turn right here staying within the park boundaries. You can relax now, as there is a boundary fence.

The path will bend to the right and a little further ahead it will veer away from the road. Stay with the wider path passing a golf course on the left, through the trees. Ignore a path on the right, now in an open grassy glade with mature beech trees. Continue straight ahead ignoring the minor paths.

When you meet with another path turn left, and on reaching a football pitch on your left you will see three paths. Take the path straight ahead and on reaching another wider path ahead turn right. **❸** Follow the stock fence on your left, and turn left onto a minor path still following with the stock fence.

Ignore a path on the left at the end of the fence line, and then ignore the immediate right path but take the right path following it. At the end of the path take an immediate left turn. There is a bank on your left. Now you need to get your dog under close control, as there is another exit ahead on to a road.

When you reach the exit, turn right, staying in the boundary of the park. A small ascent brings you into a grassy area with views of the river Mersey. **❹** You can sit for a while and enjoy the view with well spaced silver birch and gorse surrounding the area.

Continue across the grassy area towards the river and follow the worn path veering to the right. The path bends to the left and will join a sealed path parallel to the river. You will reach the far end of the car park. Depending where you have parked you can take a right path here to cross the field, keeping dogs away from the car park.

On entering another field, you will pass some picnic benches on the right and then a fenced children's play area. You will then reach the main car park. Your dog can get a drink outside the entrance for the visitor centre before going back to your car.

9. Parkgate

Medium - 4 miles - 2hrs

This is a super walk which lies partly along a section of the Wirral Way an old disused railway. There are mixed deciduous trees with scrub on each side of the path. Then you will walk along the edge of the salt marsh, where you can see across to North Wales and watch the bird life as you go. It is best to discourage dogs from entering the salt marsh as there may be ground nesting birds during the summer or over-wintering birds that need to rest before a long migratory flight. There are two small streams along the way where your dog will find water. There is only a short section of road and no livestock.

How to get there - Take the A540 from Chester signed for Heswall. Turn left on reaching the traffic lights with the Hinderton Arms on your left. Follow signs for Wirral Country Park. Stay on this road, also signed for Parkgate. The car park is found on your left on Station Road just before reaching the Cricket Club.

Grid Reference - SJ 283778
Nearest Postcode - CH64 6QJ

Parking - Free in the car park

Facilities - There are no facilities

You will need - Dog bags, dog lead and water in hot weather

The Walk

❶ From the car park go back onto the road and turn right, crossing to the other side before the bend in the road. Take the left path entering the Wirral Way, which is a disused railway.

Walking between the mixed broadleaved trees, the path bends to the left where you should ignore a path to the left and continue straight ahead. Ignore another path to the right that goes to the football fields. The Wirral Way is also popular with cyclists so make sure you keep your dog safe and under close control.

You will pass a school on your left. Cross a bridge and continue between the hedgerows and broadleaved trees. Keep to the surfaced path and not the dirt path to your right, as this is a bridleway.

After you pass houses on your left the railway embankments enclose the area, with trees and scrub to both sides. Your dog will find water here, from a stream. Pass under a road bridge and continue on the path until you reach a second road bridge.

❷ Take the steps to the right of the bridge. Once at the top turn left, following the grassy path and descending towards the estuary. There are hedgerows

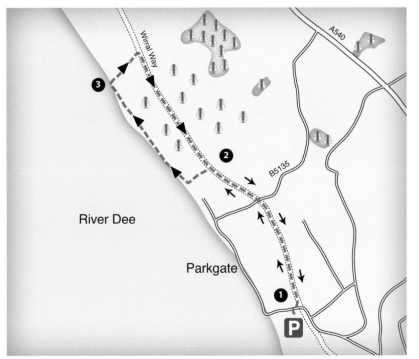

and fields on both sides of the path. Your dog will find running water to the left here. On reaching the gate pass through and turn right.

Pass through the old stone gate posts with the marsh and estuary to your left, following the gravel path with a hedgerow to your right. Cross a sleeper bridge and continue, where at the end of the hedge you will see the golf course. Ensure that your dog stays on the path and doesn't go across the golf course or down the wall to the marsh, where they will disturb over-wintering birds or ground nesting birds during April – July.

Ignore the footpath across the golf course and continue straight ahead, where you will have views across to North Wales on a clear day. There are a couple of streams flowing under the path on this section, for dogs to get water. ❸ You will reach a set of steps; putting your dog on the lead, continue down the steps and turn right onto the quiet road.

When you reach the brow of a hill, which is a road bridge across the railway, follow the footpath just beyond on the right which descends onto the Wirral Way once more, turning left on reaching the path.

Continue along the path, with estuary views through the trees to your right and the golf course to both sides over the hedgerows. Ignore the footpath to the left and continue straight on, passing under a road bridge, now following on a familiar path.

When you pass under another road bridge your dog will find water, which flows down the bank to your left. Cross over a bridge once more and continue with the embankment to both sides.

Where you see the paths split ahead put your dog on the lead and take the left path. Once you reach the road turn right, crossing after the bend. Take the footpath on the left through a kissing gate and ascend the steps into the car park.

10. Rivacre Valley

Easy - 1.4 miles - 45min

This walk is easy to follow, walking along Rivacre Brook through beautiful, deciduous woodland with meadows. You will then cross a bridge and follow through woodland back along the brook. You will encounter no roads (except for crossing one that cuts the park in two) and no livestock. Your dog will find plenty of water along the way.

How to get there - From Hooton, turn onto Hooton Green. On reaching the junction, turn left onto Hooton Lane, and then at another junction turn right onto Rivacre Road. Continue alongside the motorway at first and you will see the car park on your left at little further along.

Grid Reference - SJ 383777
Nearest Postcode - CH64 2UQ

Parking - Free in the car park (which closes at 5pm; there is a lay-by alongside)

Facilities - There are no facilities

You will need - Dog leads, dog bags

The Walk

❶ Take the path furthest from the entrance on the right hand side of the car park. Turn left and pass the wooden cabin. Cross a footbridge over a pond. In early summer the pond has lovely yellow flag iris.

On reaching a tarmac path, turn right, descending amongst the broadleaved trees. Take the path on the left, putting dogs on leads as there is a road ahead. Walking beside the river, you will pass a bridge on your right. Go through the exit just after the bridge, crossing the road.

❷ You will see an entrance back into the park. On entering the park turn right, cross a bridge and turn left. Continue along the gravel path, through the mixed deciduous woodland, alongside the river. A little further along, you will pass a bridge on your left and a path on your right. Continue following the river. You will leave the woodland to enter a large meadow on the right of the path. To the left the woodland continues on the other side of the river.

A little further along you will pass another bridge on your left and, again, a path on your right. Continue along the edge of the meadow.

❸ Take the next bridge on your left as the meadow narrows. Veer left into the woodland, now walking along the other side of the river. Continue passing a couple of bridges, and just after the path becomes tarmac once more, take a path on your left. Pass through a small open grassy area. The path then leads back into the woodland. Call your dog close as the road is near. On passing the bridge, put your dog on a lead and pass again through the exit, onto the road.

Turn back into the entrance on a familiar path, pass the bridge on the left and continue. Take the path on the right and then turn right again on the path which ascends back to the car park.

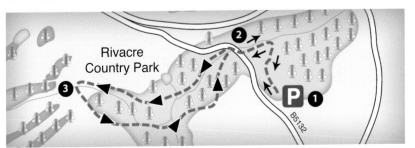

11. River Dee

Medium - 4.8 miles - 2hr 30min

This is a stunning walk in the heart of Chester. The walk follows the River Dee, where you pass through beautiful wide open meadows. Dogs love to cool off in the river on hot days. When you leave the River Dee you will pass through mixed broadleaved woodland, where your dog can run through the trees. There are short sections of road and cattle and horses graze the meadow, but they are used to dog walkers and don't show any interest in dogs. There is plenty of water along the way.

How to get there - From the A483, follow signs to Chester, passing the Chester business park on your left. On crossing the Grosvenor Bridge turn immediately right onto Castle Drive, where the car park will be on your right.

Grid Reference - SJ 404656
Nearest Postcode - CH1 1SL

Parking - Pay and Display in the Little Roodee car park – Minimum charge after 5pm

Facilities - There is a café at the far end of the car park

You will need - Dog leads, dog bags

The Walk

1 From the car park take the path alongside the river near to the entrance. Turn left onto the path, with the river to your right, beyond the trees. A sandstone wall will replace the metal fence on your right, where you will see the river below.

You will see a lovely arched bridge, ahead and to your right. At the end of the road, cross over and turn right, crossing the bride over the River Dee. Turn left immediately after crossing the bridge. **2** Descend the steps and walk beside the green on the tarmac path.

Continue on the path, beside a building on your right and the river on your left, passing the weir. After passing the building you will pass under mature trees, with willow lining the river bank. It is safe to let your dog off the lead here.

Continue on this path passing several benches and pass under a suspension bridge. You will be walking parallel to the river, passing grand houses on your right. Shortly after passing the houses you will reach black and white estate fencing, and then pass through the kissing gate next to the ornate iron gate to enter 'The Meadows'. There are a small number of cattle grazing during the summer months, but the area is very popular with dog walkers, and so the cows are used to people and

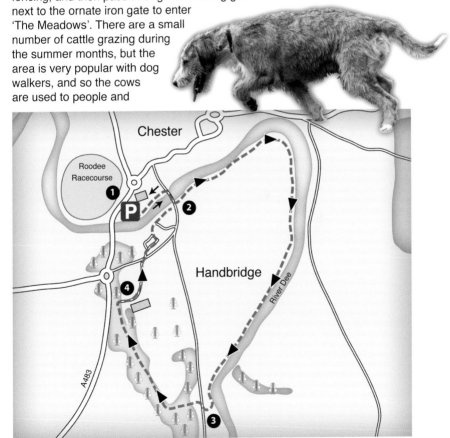

46

dogs. Make sure your dog is under close control when near the cattle.

Continue on the path beside the river, on the edge of extensive meadows with willow trees lining the path. There is an area that is cut regularly, for leisure use. The long grass has many butterflies on sunny summer days. Try to prevent your dog going into the long grass between March and July as there may be ground nesting birds.

There are places along the bank where your dog can access the water. There are grand houses on the opposite side of the river, some with fine architecture. You will eventually reach a path going right. Ignore this path and continue beside the river. After a while you will pass a ferry landing and a fenced off wetland area beside the river, with yellow flag iris and reed mace.

You will reach a path on the left where the main path bends sharply to the right. Take this path, passing through a metal kissing gate into more meadows. There are a few horses grazing here. Stay on the path, beside the river, cross a footbridge, then pass through several meadows with gaps in the hedge where gates once stood. The path is fenced off from the river in places.

Pass through another metal kissing gate; stay on the well worn, grassy path, through another meadow. Cross a footbridge and continue on the path where again you pass through several meadows, without gates.

You will pass a pumping station on the right and shortly after, you will leave the meadows. Pass a large, impressive, sandstone rock face, and then shortly after pass a couple of houses on your right.

❸ Go through another kissing gate and turn right immediately, on the worn grassy path. Pass a farm gate on your right and then pass around mature willow trees. A short ascent brings you into another field. Put your dog on a lead, as you will soon approach a busy road. Follow the hedgerow on your right and go through the kissing gate. Turn right to walk along the pavement for a short distance, and then after the farm gate on the opposite side of the road, cross the road to enter a path, into woodlands.

Once in the woodlands, ignore a narrow path on the right and continue straight ahead on a wider, worn path. Cross a few drainage ditches and then on reaching a wider path, turn left and then after a short distance you will reach a tarmac path, where you should turn right. This path is known as Duke's Drive.

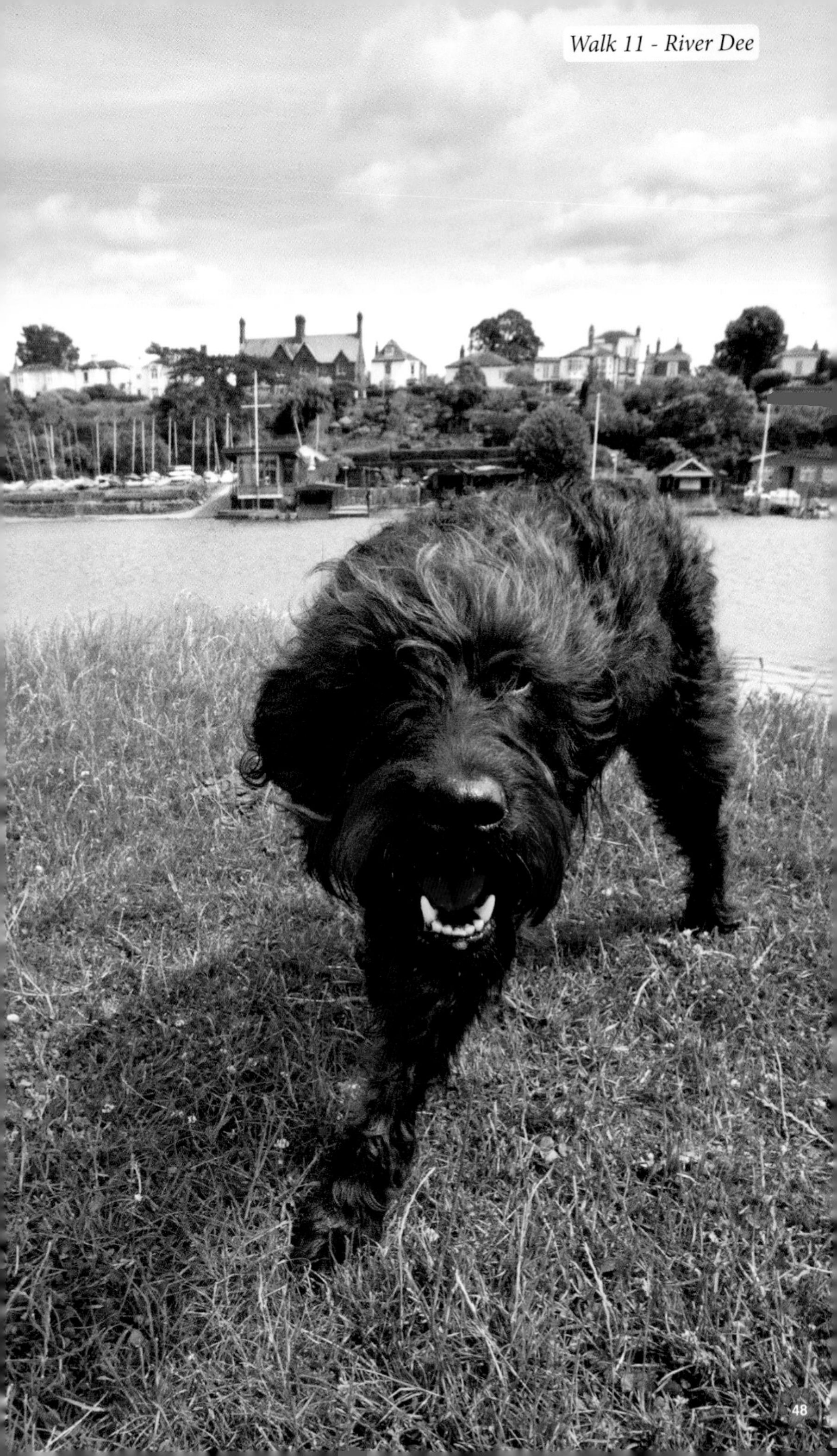

The path is wooded on either side and to begin with there are meadows on your right, through the trees. Stay on the path, where your dogs will be free to run in and out of the trees. Ignore paths to the left and to the right and continue straight ahead. After a while you will see a busy road ahead. Before reaching the road there are more paths to the left and right. Putting dogs on leads, take the path on the right, beside a field, passing through the kissing gate onto a quiet road. ❹ You will pass a Catholic high school on your right, where you can walk along the pavement.

Cross a side street and continue on the old Wrexham road. On reaching a busy road, cross at the pelican crossing and turn right. Take the next road on the left and pass the cottages. When reaching Westminster Green, walk alongside the green with houses on your right. Turn left at the end of the green and follow the green, now on your left. After passing the houses on your right, take the footpath on your right.

Descend the steps and go through the gate into a horse paddock, keeping dogs under close control. Go straight ahead, crossing the field and go through another kissing gate. On reaching a path turn right. Go into Edgar's Field Park, which parallels the River Dee. Pass the sandstone outcrop on your right.

Follow the tarmac path, ensuring your dog is on the lead. Pass the children's play area on your left and take the exit out of the park onto Handbridge Road, turning left. You will see the familiar road bridge ahead. Cross the road, and continue over the bridge.

Once across the bridge, cross back to the other side and go straight ahead on the road that parallels the River Dee, back to the car park.

12. Helsby

Medium - 2 miles - 1hr

This is a wonderful walk with fantastic panoramic views, which are breathtaking as far as the eye can see, beautiful broadleaved woodland, quiet country lanes and some heathland, gorse and sandstone outcrops. There is a little section of quiet road and no livestock to worry about.

How to get there - From the M56 junction 14 follow signs for Helsby. On passing the Community Sports Centre on the A56 Chester road take the right hand turn, following the brown signs for Helsby Quarry.

Grid Reference - SJ 490749
Nearest Postcode - WA6 9PT

Parking - Free at Helsby Quarry car park

Facilities - There are no facilities

You will need - Dog leads, dog bags and water for your dog

The Walk

❶ From the car park at the furthest end from the road, take the pedestrian exit and cross the road to ascend Hill Road South. Go through the gateway and the gap between fencing to enter Helsby Hill.

Continue straight ahead on the worn path through mixed broadleaved woodland. There is a heavily vegetated rocky outcrop to your right and there are lots of ferns on the woodland floor.

You will reach a fork on the path ahead. Take the left path which is signed Helsby Hilltop. Ascend the sandstone steps and continue walking, with a stock fence to your right to begin with.

As you climb above the tree line keep your dog under close control, as there are cliff edges. You will be amazed at the views that unfold before you - views which stretch as far as the eye can see.

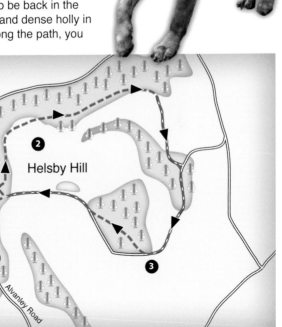

❷ Pass the trig point with the cliff faces to your left, and continue straight on to the corner of a fence line ahead. Follow the worn path, which descends with a few steps veering to the left and then has a sharp bend to the right.

You will have more views straight ahead across to the Peak District. Descend the sandstone steps, soon to be back in the woods with lots of ferns and dense holly in places. A little further along the path, you

Helsby Hill

will meet with another fork; take the path on the right that ascends a little at first.

Descending now with a few steps, pass the stile with a gap for dogs and turn right following the path signed Hill Road North. You will walk past a farm gate and between stock fencing, passing under a line of mature horse chestnut trees in the hedgerow, with hills and fields to both sides.

Before reaching the end of the lane put your dog on the lead and pass the houses on your right. There is a sandstone outcrop to your left. When you meet with another quiet road turn right. There are fields and horse paddocks on either side.

The road ascends a little and you will reach a parking bay on the right, with an entrance to Harmers Wood. ❸ Go into the wood and take the path on the left. When you meet a fork take the left path, and then a right fork to pass a quarry on your left. Stay to the left of the wood and continue through the oak and silver birch trees. When you meet with another path put your dog on the lead, and turn left where you will exit the woods.

Turn right on the road, and before reaching the entrance to a farmhouse take the lane on the left following the sign for Helsby Hill. You will walk between fields, passing Harmer's Lake on your right over the other side of the hedge. On reaching the end of the lane ignore the right turn and continue straight ahead where the path narrows.

Continue between the hedgerows, descending between exposed sandstone. You will soon be on a familiar path veering left to continue your descent, putting your dog back on the lead before going back out through the barrier and down the road to your car.

13. Frodsham

Medium - 3.4 miles - 2hrs

Taking in part of the Sandstone Trail and passing beside a large stretch of sandstone outcrop, this walk has everything: breathtaking views that reach as far as the eye can see across flat lands, beautiful oak and silver birch woodland, quiet country lanes, farmland and woodland valleys. A descent down a path known as Jacob's Ladder brings you into a fantastic dell surrounded by rock faces and mature oak trees. There is a little bit of climbing back up with one or two large sandstone steps that an old arthritic dog would struggle with. There are small sections of road without pavements and you may encounter livestock as you cross through farmland.

How to get there - From the direction of Helsby go through Frodsham town centre, and turn right at the traffic lights onto the B5152 following the brown signs for Forest Hills Hotel. Further on, turn right following Forest Hills Hotel and Manley. Turn right onto Simons Lane where you will see signs for Frodsham Golf Course, and on passing the Golf Course the car park will be on the right hand side.

Grid Reference - SJ 518765 **Nearest Postcode** - WA6 6HE

Parking - Free in the Beacon Hill car park

Facilities - There are no facilities

You will need - Dog lead, dog bags and water for your dog

Countryside Dog Walks - Wirral & West Cheshire

The Walk

❶ Dogs will need to be on a lead to begin with. From the car park go back out onto the road and turn left. The road descends with fields on the left and gardens on the right. Once passing the horse paddock on the left take the driveway for Overhill Cottage. You will now have the horse paddock to your left.

Just as you enter the front garden of the house to your left, keep to the right hand side and follow between the holly and hawthorn hedgerow. You will reach a sealed road; cross this and take the path straight ahead.

Now walk between the laurel and stock fence, with nice views to the right where the trees allow. Pass the field on the right, and then the area will open out a little with a garden to your left and houses below the hill on the right.

On reaching a road turn right on a decline, and when at the bend in the road, you will pass the Belle Monte Hotel on your left. Turn left into the car park and immediately after the hotel take the footpath to your right. Then take the immediate path on the left.

This will bring you into lovely woodland, following the worn path, which cuts across

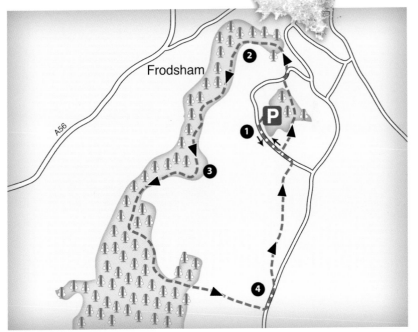

the hillside. You are now on part of the long distance path the Sandstone Trail.

You will meet two paths ahead. Take the path on the left signed for Delamere and Beeston. The path inclines with exposed sandstone and lots of ferns. Take the steps on the left where you will reach a war memorial. The views here will astound you, with a 180 degree panorama as far as the eye will allow.

❷ Pass the war memorial on your left and continue, passing a small field on your left with gorse and trees to your right. You will meet with two paths further ahead. Take the right, lower path.

With exposed rock on your left, the path cuts into the wooded hillside known as Frodsham Hill Wood. Again the woodland is dominated by oak and silver birch, and holly understory with lots of ferns on the woodland floor.

You will reach some impressive sandstone rocks - just before them, ignore a set of steps to the left. On reaching the outcrops ignore steps both to the left and right, continuing with the rock face to your left. Just after passing a sign for Frodsham Hill Wood, ignore a path on the left, pass a way marker, then veer left over the sandstone outcrop.

Continue following the edge of the hill, where you leave the sandstone behind and the woodland opens up with rhododendron to your right. You will now have fields and gorse to your left and a gap in the woodland provides you with a view, when you reach a bench.

You will reach a golf course on your left as the path begins to descend. Ignore the path on the left signed for Beacon Hill car park that cuts across the golf course, and turn right descending the steps. Stay on the path with the fence to your left and descend, with a series of steps known as Jacob's Ladder.
❸ You will see the sandstone to your left once more.

At the bottom of the steps, now in a fantastic wooded dell surrounded by sandstone and mature oak trees, turn right and on reaching another path turn left signed Delamere.

The path ascends now with ferns and woodrush covering the woodland floor. Cross a footbridge and turn right heading towards another sandstone outcrop, which is gnarly. As you reach the rock you will see the hidden steps. Once at the top you will see the golf course to your left once more, and views to your right where the trees allow.

There is exposed sandstone bedrock once more along the path. When you pass the end of the golf course continue ahead, taking care with your dog as the exposed rock ahead has a cliff face. You will still be walking in oak and silver birch woodland, with rhododendron bushes to both sides of the path.

Take the path on the left, signed Sandstone Trail, which ascends with some steps. You will meet with an old stone wall on your right. Cross the wall at the footpath indicator to then have the wall on your left. The path bends to the right and you will have farmland on your left, as you walk through the edge of the woodland.

At the end of the farmland the path veers left, still following the edge of the field. Ignore a path on the right and now you will leave the Sandstone Trail behind. Continue straight on entering Snidley Moor Wood. Just after the end of farm fields on your left the path splits in two. Take the right path ascending the steps.

You will pass a path on the right and then a path on the left continuing straight ahead. Leaving the woods behind and walk between farmland with a hedgerow to your right. Put your dog on a lead and pass through the gate, and then continue along the lane passing houses on the left and right.

❹ On reaching the road turn left, walking with care as cars pass with speed and there is no footpath. Walk along the grass verge, keeping dogs in, as they usually have a tendency to pull to the road.

Pass through the metal kissing gate and cross the field diagonally right, heading for the satellite pylon ahead. There are views to the left over the estuary. Pass through another kissing gate, descending the steps to cross a farm track, and go back up the steps to follow on the narrow path with barbed fence to the left and wire fencing to the right.

Pass the golf course again to your left and horse paddocks to the right. Ignore a stile on the right and continue. You will enter the putting area of the golf course. Ensure your dog is on the lead and follow the hedgerow on the left, and continue passing a couple of gates to the end, where you meet with the road.

Cross the road with care and walk facing the on-coming traffic; again there is no footpath so keep your dog pulled in close. You will soon recognise where you are as you pass the entrance to Overhill Cottage. A little further on pass the horse paddock and you will soon see the car park on the right.

14. Delamere Forest   Easy - 3.2 miles - 1hr 30min

This forest walk is ideal for dogs, having very little road and no livestock. It has streams where your dog can get a drink and a lake walk where dogs can take a dip to cool off. There are some broadleaved trees amongst the coniferous forest and you can enjoy a coffee half way round at the café, which has an outside seating area. It's an ideal walk in hot weather. There may be cyclists and horses on sections of this walk.

How to get there - From Chester follow the A51 signed for Nantwich, turning onto the A54 for Tarvin, and then take the A556 signed for Northwich. On reaching the Vale Royal Abby Arms turn left, following the brown signs for Delamere. Then ignore the sign for Delamere visitor centre and train station and continue into Hatchmere, turning left once in the village, at the cross roads, and a little further on the car park will be on the left hand side.

Grid Reference - SJ 541715
Nearest Postcode - WA6 6PB

Parking - Free in the Forestry Commission car park

Facilities - There is a visitor centre, toilets, a cafe and a shop half way around the walk

You will need - Dog leads, dog bags

The Walk

❶ Go to the end of the car park furthest from the road and follow the path, which bends left and meets a wider track. Continue forward on this track, which is part of the Sandstone Trail, through mixed broadleaved trees.

You will pass a boggy pond to your left, ignore a path on your right and then pass a path to your left. You will meet another path, which crosses the path that you are on. Go straight ahead here. Pass a wet area to your right and then at the bend take the path to the left.

❷ Cross the railway bridge and ignore two paths to your right. There is a stream to the right where your dog will find water. Just a little further on turn left, leaving the sandstone trail to follow on the Baker Way.

The path descends at first and then ascends quite steeply, passing another stream at the dip in the hill. You will pass a thicket of young regeneration to both sides of the path, and then continue into a forest of Scots pine and larch.

Ignore a path to the left that goes over a bridge and continue straight ahead,

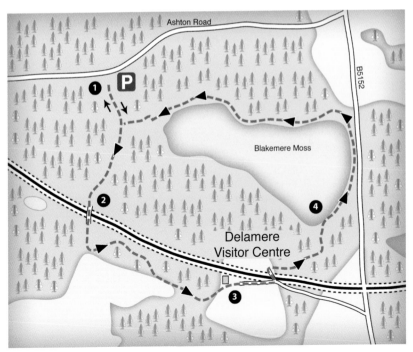

descending now towards the edge of the forest with fields to your right. Pass another wet area on the left and continue straight ahead with the forest to your left. The path will bend to the left.

At the end of the field, ensure you have your dog on a lead as you near an overflow car park to your right. Once you reach a track turn left with the car park on your right. Continue on the narrow path, parallel to the sealed road and when you pass a house on the left, join a path to the left, which leads to the visitor centre, toilets, café and shop.

❸ Continue passing the main car park on your left, making use of the paths to get off the road. You will pass the warden's station on the right and then ascend to the railway bridge on the left. Cross the railway and take a path on the right, just before reaching a house to the left. You will pass a path on the left and the Go Ape cabin on the right. Follow on this path where you will reach the lake, Blakemere Moss.

❹ Once reaching another path at the lake turn right, staying on this path, which follows near to the water's edge. Be aware ahead as you will come near to the roadside on your right. Keep your dog under close control or on a lead when near to the road as there are no boundary fences; you will see daylight ahead as you approach.

Pass an entrance into the forest as you near the road and continue to follow with the lake. Further on, the path will have a sharp bend to the left where you pass a path on your right. You will stay with the lake and leave the road behind once more, where it is safe to let your dog off the lead.

You will pass benches where you can take a rest and enjoy the lakeside. Ignore a path on the right and continue straight ahead. The path will bend sharply to the right, where you will leave the lake. Ignore another path on the right a little further along and continue on the main path, which bends to the left. You will see the lake beyond the silver birch trees.

When you see a path on the left and the right, take the dirt path to the right, passing a picnic bench to your right, and keep to the left amongst the broadleaved trees, following the path between the embankments. On reaching another path turn right and then ignore a path on the left; you will pass a familiar boggy pond to your right. Ignore a minor path to the right and then take the next right back to the car park.

15. Marbury Park

Medium - 4 miles - 2hr

This is a delightful circular walk with wonderful woodlands, a beautiful mere, lots of lovely meadows and a canal walk to the Anderton Boat lift, where you can enjoy a pub lunch at the dog friendly Stanley Arms. Then it returns on a different route passing extensive meadows and woodland, with an impressive lime avenue. Your dog will enjoy running through the trees and across the meadows, finding water at several points along the way.

How to get there - From Northwich, follow the signs to Anderton Boat Lift and Marbury Country Park. Continue past the boat lift to follow signs for Marbury Park.

Grid Reference - SJ 650765
Postcode - CW9 6AT

Parking - Pay and display

Facilities - There are toilets and a covered sitting area

You will need - Dog leads, dog bags

The Walk

❶ Facing the ticket machine, go to your left and follow the edge of the car park. Leave the car park, pass a meadow on your right and go through a gate, then turn left. Take the path on the left of the toilet block. Pass between trees and lawn areas. Ignore a path on your left.

The path becomes tarmac; on meeting another path, turn right. The path will bend to the right and you will see Budworth Mere on your left through the trees. Turn left to descend the wide, sandstone steps. On reaching the bird hide, turn right to follow the water's edge, with mixed broadleaved trees on your right.

You may either take the steps on the left, which pass the boathouse, or stay on the wider path under the trees; both paths join ahead. Continue alongside the mere until the path veers away to the right.

Pass a fenced-off pond on your right and ignore a path on the right that leads to the bird hide. Ignore several paths on your left and continue with the wider path through the woodland. When you reach a fork turn left, following the sign to Anderton Nature Park.

Stay on the main path, ignoring any desire lines. After a while you will pass near to the edge of farmland, staying on the main path through the woods.

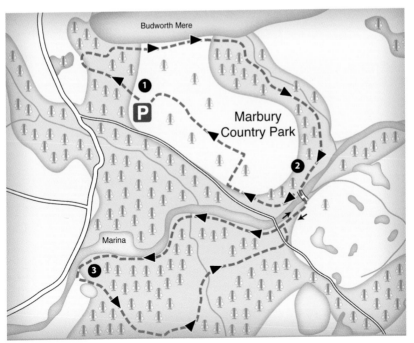

❷ You will eventually reach a bridge; cross this over the canal. Continue straight ahead, between the hedges, parallel with the canal on your right.

Where the path bends sharply to your right, take a path on the left. You will now be on the tow path, where you turn left. Follow beside the canal, where you will reach the marina. When you approach the marina, it may be better to have dogs on leads, as it may be busy here with people mooring boats and there is a road ahead. Cross a bridge and go back onto the tow path.

Just beyond the marina, you will reach the Anderton boat lift. There is a dog friendly pub here, The Stanley Arms, if you choose to stop for a pub lunch or a coffee. Turn back, passing the boat lift once more, towards the marina, but on reaching the bridge take the steps on the right, **❸** ensuring your dog is on a lead.

Cross an access road and continue straight ahead, passing a couple of fishing ponds on your right. Watch out for cars entering the parking bays ahead. There may be horses on this path. Ignore a path on the right and pass beside a vehicle barrier. A little further along the area opens out with meadows and wooded areas. Take the path on the left, into Uplands Woodland. This is a large meadow, surrounded by trees. Follow the path with the meadow on your right.

Ignore a path on the right and continue straight ahead. The path veers to the left as you leave the meadow. Cross a bridge over the river, and then, ascending a little, you will pass a meadow on your right. Ascend a little once more, and then the area opens up, with lovely meadows to your left. Ignore a path on the right and a little further ahead, you will reach a tarmac path. Cross this path to enter Dairy House Meadow. Turn left after going through the kissing gate. Ignore a path on the left and continue on a familiar path, where you cross back over the bridge to the other side of the canal.

Turn left, where you will now find yourself back in the woodlands of Marbury Park. Follow alongside the canal on your left to begin with, and then the path will bend sharply to the right, leaving the canal. Ignore a path on your left and continue straight ahead. You will come near to farmland on your right. Stay on the wider, woodland path.

On reaching another path, turn right, walking between farmland, with a hedgerow on your right and stock fence on your left. Go through the kissing gate on your left and follow the path through the middle of the field (there may be cattle grazing). Pass through the kissing gate on the other side, into silver birch woodland. You will pass a lovely flower meadow on your left. On meeting another path, cross this to go straight ahead. There is an impressive lime avenue on your right. You can walk between the lime avenue or stay on the path. Take the next path on the left, passing the interpretation panel and returning to the car park.

16. Bickerton Hill

Medium - 3.4 miles - 1hr 40min

This is a spectacular walk with a mixture of habitats, including mixed broadleaved woodland, silver birch woodland, and heathland, with lots of bilberry, gorse and meadows. There is even an Iron Age hill fort - from this site you will have amazing views over the Cheshire plains. This is a fantastic place to take your dog. During the nesting season, however, it is required that you keep dogs on a lead or under very close control, so to get the best out of this walk perhaps visit from 1st August to 28th February. In August you will get the best out of the stunning heathland, as it will be in full bloom. There are ponies grazing on the heathland.

How to get there - Take the A41 from Chester signed Whitchurch. At the Broxton roundabout turn left, following for Nantwich, and then take the next turn on your right signed for Duckington. Take the third left turn on an unmarked, narrow road and the car park will be reached at the top.

Grid Reference - SJ 494525

Parking - Free in Duckington car park

Facilities - There are no facilities

You will need - Dog leads, dog bags and water for your dog

The Walk

1 From the car park, pass the interpretation panel on the main path, and continue through the mixed broadleaved woodland with farmland on your left. Ignore a right turn and continue to the edge of the woodland. The path begins to ascend.

Pass through a gate and continue straight ahead on a red, sandy path with some exposed bedrock. On reaching a plateau, ignore a path on your right and continue straight ahead. Silver birch dominates the woodland on your right.

The path will descend now. Pass through another gate and take the path on the right, passing an interpretation panel. Again, pass through a gate and continue straight ahead, where you leave the woods to enter into partial heathland with bilberry and silver birch regeneration.

As the path veers to the right, turn onto a path on your left. Ignore a narrow path on the left, and then on reaching another path back into the woods turn left. Follow the path through silver birch woodland. Continue on this path, straight ahead, until you reach another path, close to stock fencing. When you reach this path, turn right. You will reach a few steps, near to the corner of the stock fence.

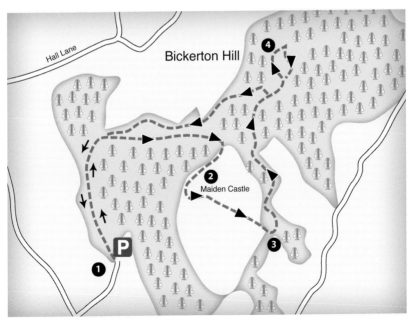

Ascend the steps, where you will have the stock fence on your left continuing on an upward climb. Another set of steps helps you up the steeper section of the hill. As you climb you will have views to your left.

Just as the path you are on begins to descend quite sharply, you will see a distinct path on your right. Take this path, to continue on an upward climb. The trees will become widely spaced and you will meet another broader path. Turn right here and take the path with the steps. Continue straight ahead, still ascending, with another set of stone steps. You will now have views to your right, where trees allow, and heathland to your left. A little further along the area opens up with extensive views. ❷ On a clear day, you can see across to Liverpool and the Clwydian Range in North Wales. You are now at the site of the Maiden Castle hill fort.

Continue on to descend the stone steps and turn left staying on the gravel path. To your left you can see the castle ramparts. Pass through the heathland, with scattered trees. Ignore a path to your left and continue along the edge of the heath on your right, with woodland with heather understory on your left. You will pass a meadow on your right. On reaching a gate, do not go through it, but take the path on your left, staying within the boundaries. ❸

You will reach another grassy path: turn left here through the woods. The path veers to the left, once you are near to a field. You will now follow parallel to the field edge on your right. You will have views to your right, where the trees allow. The woods are dominated by silver birch with bracken understory. You will follow around three sides of the field edge and then near to the middle of the field the path will veer to the left.

You will reach a sunken path. Turn right here, and on reaching another path, turn right again. To your left here, you will see a familiar path with steps, but

you will now be going in the opposite direction. Pass through an area with widely spaced trees and heather and bilberry coving the ground. Ignore a right turn and continue straight ahead, ascending through another sunken path, which is part of the Sandstone Trail.

Just as you near the top of the ascent, take the path on the left, signed Rawhead/Beeston. To your right is a sandstone block with an interpretation panel. Continue on the Sandstone Trail, with a wooded slope on your left and heathland on your right. Keep dogs under close control, as there is a cliff edge. You will be met with outstanding views on your left, across the Cheshire Plain. ❹

Continue on this path with views to your left, passing Kitty's Stone, and then enter back into silver birch woodland. The path descends, and just before passing 'The Slars', which is the sandstone rock face ahead and to your right, take the path on the right. You will pass a field edge, and then staying on the grassy path amongst the trees and heathland you will reach a gate on the left. Turn right here, heading back towards the sandstone block

with an interpretation panel. Go back along the sunken path and then turn immediately right, along a grassy path.

On reaching a fork, take the path on the left, descending on the sandstone bedrock between bracken and bilberry. Cutting across the wooded slope, you will reach a kissing gate. Don't go through it, but turn left. The path ascends, with a stock fence on your right. Pass some exposed rock face on your left, and then descend and ignore a path on your left. Descend a set of steps. You will then reach the corner of the stock fence and descend the steps on a familiar path. Turn immediately right here, to continue with the stock fence.

Ignore a path on your left and continue with the field edge, passing a boggy area to your left. Follow this path through the woodlands for some time. You will reach an enclosed area with goal posts. Continue on the path and on reaching a gate on your right, pass through it on to a familiar path. Pass through another gate, and descend the gradual slope. Ignore a path to the left and continue to retrace your steps back to the car park.

17. Little Budworth

Easy - 2 miles - 1hr

This is a wonderful woodland walk with quiet sandy paths and pockets of heathland, passing alongside farmland and a lovely pond with a ring of yellow flag iris in early summer. Close to Oulton Park racetrack, you may hear the sound of racing cars. There are no roads, other than crossing over a couple of quiet lanes.

How to get there - Take the A51 from Chester following in the direction of Nantwich and Winsford. Turn onto the A54, signed for Winsford. At the traffic lights turn right onto the A49 following signs for Tarporley and Oulton Park. Turn left onto Coach Road, following signs for Little Budworth. Near to the end of the road, turn left into the car park.

Grid Reference - SJ 590654
Nearest Postcode - CW6 9EE

Parking - Free in the car park

Facilities - There are toilets in the car park

You will need - Dog leads, dog bags and water for your dog

Countryside Dog Walks - Wirral & West Cheshire

The Walk

❶ Take the entrance between the interpretation panels and follow the well-worn path into mixed broadleaved trees. The path bends to the right, where you ignore a path on the right.

Walking with a field edge on your right, stay on the path close to the woodland edge. A little further along, a laurel hedge encloses The White Hall on your right. Pass through a gap next to a gate and continue along the path, now moving deeper into the woods.

Cross an access drive to the hall and continue straight ahead. There is lots of bracken covering the woodland floor. Cross a bridleway and continue on the well-worn path. The woodland is mainly silver birch, oak and rowan understory here.

Ignore a path on your left and then almost immediately take a path on your right, following the purple way markers. Ignore paths on the left and right and continue straight ahead, following the woodland edge once more. **❷** A little further along, you will pass a pond on the left, just as you reach the edge of a field on your right.

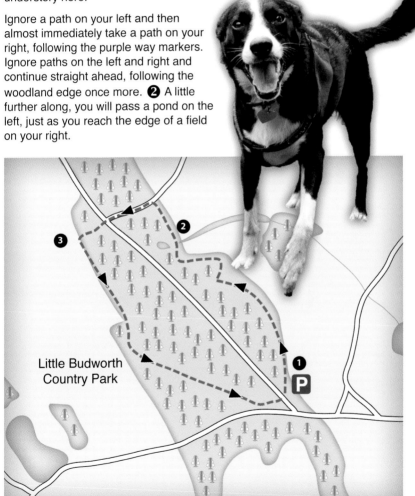

Little Budworth
Country Park

Turn left just after the pond, following the purple arrow. Ascend a set of steps, and follow the path. Brambles now dominate the woodland floor. Ignore a path on your right, staying on the main path. There is a road below and to your far left, so keep your dog under close control, as there are no boundary fences.

The woods will clear where you cross a small heath. After crossing the heath, pass through a gap next to a gate, back into the woods. Stay on the main path, keeping your dog under close control, as there is a quiet road ahead. Before reaching the road put your dog on a lead. Once at the road turn left, where you will meet another road. Cross this and take the by-way on the opposite side. Ignore a path on your left. Keep dogs under close control as horses and farm vehicles use this sandy track.

❸ Take a path on the left, signed to Smithy Lane, where you will pick up the purple arrow once more. Ignore a path on the left almost immediately and continue, following another field boundary to the woodland edge. You will see heathland on your far left, through the trees. Stay on the main path, following the field boundary. Pass through a gap in the post and rail fence. At the end of the field, you will reach a fork ahead. Take the path to the left and continue to follow the purple way markers. This path is also a bridleway, therefore you may encounter horses.

Continue along the sandy path, where you will pass another small heathland pocket on your right beyond the trees. A little further along you will cross another bridlepath. Ignore a footpath on the left and continue straight ahead. On reaching a clearing, keep your dog under close control, as there is a road close by.

Ignore a footpath on the left and continue, where you will pass through another small heathland pocket in the woodland clearing. Ignore a path on your left and put your dog on a lead. Continue, taking the next left to cross a road, following the sign to the car park.

18. Whitegate Way

Easy - 2.5 miles - 1hr 20min

This walk follows part of the old disused railway, which starts at Winsford and ends at Cuddington. It passes between farmland, and is lined with trees on both sides. There is a loop that skirts around the edge of a beautiful mere, with glimpses of the mere through the trees. The path is shared throughout with horses and cyclists.

How to get there - Take the A51 from Chester signed for Nantwich and Winsford, and then turn on the A54 signed for Winsford. After passing the Shrewsbury Arms take the next left turn signed Whitegate Way. The car park will be found on the right hand side of the road a little further along.

Grid Reference - SJ 615679
Nearest Postcode - CW7 2PB

Parking - Free in the car park

Facilities - There are toilets in the car park

You will need - Dog leads, dog bags and water for your dog

The Walk

❶ From the car park enter the Whitegate Way, turning left. Pass the old platform and train station on your left. Pass under the road bridge and continue following the wide path.

You will pass farm gates on your left and right. Here you can take a narrow path on your right, which follows along the railway embankment. Horses and cyclists don't use this path, but there are no fences so your dog can still get onto the main railway path.

You will now be walking beside the boundary to the field on your right, with trees and scrub to your left. You will pass a path that goes back onto the disused railway. Continue on, where you will pass a kissing gate and old concrete ladder stile on your right. Continue along the path, between the trees.

Pass a farm gate and continue straight ahead - the path is now level with the railway line. You will reach a track, with houses, on the other side of the fence on your right. Then, after passing palisade fencing, you will reach woodland to your right.

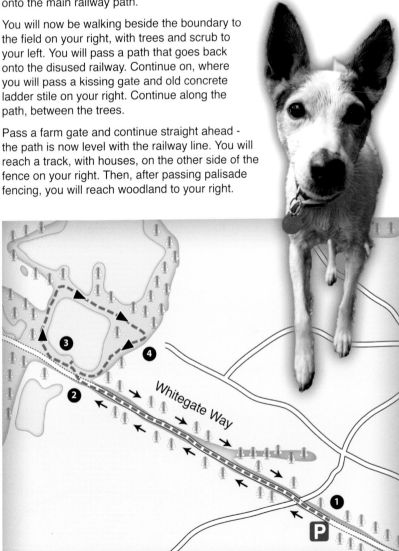

The path merges with the main railway line again and you will pass a vehicle barrier. ❷ Take the path on the right, passing beside a gate into Newchurch Common. Ignore a path to the right and take the path on the left over a stile. Your dog will get under the vehicle barrier (if you have a large breed of dog and he can't get under the barrier, go back onto the railway line and continue to the next exit on your right).

Continue along the path, which is narrow in places. When you see a path on your right, take this as a detour to have a glimpse of the large, beautiful mere. Then return to the path and turn right, to continue. The path follows parallel with the railway line for a short time.

On meeting an opening back onto the railway, turn right towards the mere. (Again, if you have a large breed of dog, after passing through the exit in the post and rail fencing continue straight ahead towards the mere).

❸ You can stand here for a while, watching the wildfowl on the water. Veer left now to re-join the path. Continue straight ahead, with the mere to your right. Listen out for fishermen's cars and keep your dog under close control. Continue straight ahead, with farmland on your left and the mere below to your right. Pine trees line the path on both sides and you will have glimpses of the mere where the trees allow.

Follow the path as it takes a sharp right turn and then pass beside the vehicle barrier to your left. Turn right on this path and continue between the trees. Have your dog under close control, as there may be cars on this path. There is a mere on each side, through the trees. ❹

You will pass a vehicle barrier on your right, and then on your left. Then pass a footpath on your left and right. Continue on the same path until you see a path on your right, which back-tracks. Take this path. After passing a field on your left, you will pass gardens and then woodland. There is woodland to your right and to the far right lies the mere. You will come close to the mere for a short spell.

You will reach a familiar path; turn left and go back through the entrance onto the Whitegate Way. Turn left here to retrace your steps back to the car park.

19. Little Leigh

Easy - 2.2 miles - 1hr 20min

This is a lovely peaceful circular walk, first passing between hedgerows with adjacent farmland, then along the quiet village road of Little Leigh onto an old cobble path, again between farmland. You will finish alongside the Trent and Mersey canal, passing the colourful narrow boats. The walk is surrounded by farmland and trees line most of the way. After leaving the shade of the trees for the last section of the canal you will see meadow flowers, with some orchids in early summer. There are no livestock and only short sections of quiet road.

How to get there - From Northwich take the A533, following signs for Runcorn. On reaching the A49, turn left, following signs for Whitchurch and Weaverham. On reaching the Leigh Arms pub turn left before going over the road bridge, onto Willow Green Lane. Continue on this road, and just after passing over the road bridge park on the left hand side in the parking bay.

Grid Reference - SJ 607759
Nearest Postcode - CW8 4QT

Parking - Free in the parking bay

Facilities - There are no facilities

You will need - Dog leads, dog bags

The Walk

❶ From the parking bay, walk back down the road and take the path on the left, before going over the bridge. This path inclines with a hedgerow and farmland on your right and woodland to your left. Keep your dog under close control as there is a road a little to your left at first, and the path ahead is also used by farm vehicles.

Continue to ascend, and you will soon have farmland on both sides, with barbed wire fencing. The path levels out and widens as you pass the farm gate on your right and you will now have hedgerows on both sides. Continue straight ahead, but keep your dog under close control, as there is a quiet lane ahead. You will see the houses and the village church steeple ahead of you.

Put your dog on the lead before reaching the end of the track. On reaching the quiet country lane turn right. Pass Church Farm on your left. Stay on Church Road, as it bends sharply to the left, passing the church on your left. Pass several houses and then take the footpath on the right, just as you pass Weaver Bank. **❷**

Follow the grassy lane, between the hedgerows, with agricultural land on either side. Mature standard trees line the right hand side of

the path. Pass through a gateway and continue. Wild flowers line the path on the right hand side. The path will have a sharp bend to the left, just as you reach a farm gate.

Continue along the path, now with old cobbles underfoot. Keep your dog under close control or on a lead now. You will pass through a gateway into the garden of a house on your right. Continue straight ahead, to follow on the cobble driveway.

On reaching the quiet lane turn right, crossing the bridge, and then turn immediately right. ❸ On meeting with the towpath turn left. There are fields on your left and the path is lined with trees.

Continue following the canal on your right for some time under the canopy of trees. Look out ahead for a circular wall to the left, which is covered in ivy, just as the canal bends to the left. Keep inquisitive dogs under close control as you pass, as it is a bridge with a drop on the other side!

In the spring and summer months there are many flowers when you leave the shade of the trees to add colour along the way, with butterflies and bees busily collecting nectar. You will pass under a lovely stone arched bridge.

Continue for some time, where you will pass the mooring for the colourful narrow boats. Just after the mooring you will pass under a bridge. Keep dogs on a lead immediately after the bridge, and take the path on the left, which leads to the quiet road. Turn left onto the road and proceed uphill, back to your car.

20. River Weaver

Easy - 3 miles - 1hr 20min

This is a fabulous circular walk, walking firstly along quiet paths amongst farmland, and then between the River Weaver on your right and a beautiful, small lake on your left. There is plenty of birdlife, and in summer, lots of yellow flag iris, damselflies and dragonflies. You will be walking through broadleaved woodland, which gives a little shade on hot, sunny days. There are no roads and only a short section where there is the possibility of livestock.

How to get there - From Northwich take the A556 and then the A533 following signs for Winsford. After the second roundabout look for the signs for Moulton on your right. Follow this turn-off, and turn left on reaching the mini roundabout. Continue passing shops and the road will narrow. At the end of this road, park on the right hand side opposite the houses.

Grid Reference - SJ 651688
Nearest Postcode - CW9 8PL

Parking - Free in car park

Facilities - There are no facilities on this walk

You will need - Dog lead, dog bags

The Walk

❶ From the car park, face the fields at the end of the road and take the path on your right, signed Northwich. There may be cyclists and horses on this path. Walk on the cinder path, between farmland, with stock fencing on both sides. A little further along the stock fence is replaced by hawthorn hedgerows.

Pass a horse paddock on your right and farm fields on your left. The path opens out, where you will meet with a junction. Ignore the path on your right, signed Northwich, and take the path on the left. Continue between the hedgerows. Once you see a bridge ahead, call your dog close to ensure that he doesn't wander onto the railway, and cross over the bridge.

Keep your dog under close control and pass through the gap beside the farm gate, walking on the well-trodden path through the middle of farmland, which is surrounded by trees. As you near the other side of the field the path will descend to a kissing gate.

❷ Pass through the kissing gate, where you will be met with the beautiful, canalised section of the River

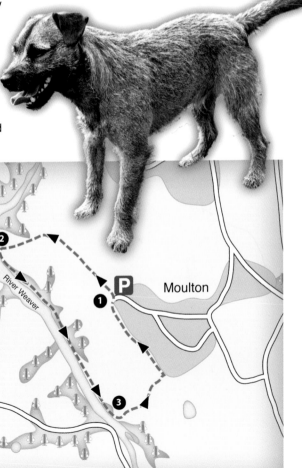

Weaver. Take the path on the left, following beside the River Weaver, with trees lining both sides. You will pass through a kissing gate, continuing on the path. Take care that your dog doesn't get too far ahead as there are cyclists on this path, and if your dog goes in the canal there are places where he may struggle to get back out.

There is lots of birdlife along the way, such as cormorants, mallards, coots, black-headed gulls and swallows, safe from dogs on the banks on the opposite side of the river. Continue on this path; a little further along you will also have wet areas on your left, with yellow flag iris in early summer. The wet areas will become a small lake, where in the summer months you will see damselfly and dragonfly. Your dog can get water here.

At the end of the lake you will leave the woodland and pass through another kissing gate. Keep your dog under close control, as there may be cattle on this section of the walk. You will enter into a grassy scrubby area on your left, then a grassland bank. You will soon pass through a kissing gate, where to your left the landscape will become wooded once more, with trees lining the river's edge.

As you see a bridge across the river ahead, call your dogs close, as you will be entering into a car park. ❸ Take the path on the left, passing through the car park, and then turn left on the footpath signed for Northwich. Ascend with woodland on both sides. Your dog will find water from a stream on your right, just before passing the drive for Vale Royal River Park.

Go through a couple of tunnels, passing under the railway. Ignore a path on your right and continue between the farmland with stock fencing on each side. Call your dog close as you near the houses ahead. On reaching a road turn left onto the cinder path. Pass houses on your right and farmland on your left.

Keep your dog under close control, as there are gaps in the fence where he may wander into gardens. You may also meet with cyclists on this path. There may be sheep grazing on the farmland and the fence is low in places, allowing a determined dog to jump over.

Continue along this path until you see the road on the left, where you have parked your car.